THE POISONER'S GARDEN & OTHERS

Selected Poems

DOUGLAS CLEGG

ALKEMARA
PRESS

Get Douglas Clegg's Newsletter

Get book updates, price drop news flashes,
and exclusive offers—become a V.I.P. member
of Douglas Clegg's long-running email
newsletter:

http://DouglasClegg.com/newsletter

Also by Douglas Clegg

Want signed and inscribed editions?
Visit DouglasClegg.com/signed-books

STAND-ALONE NOVELS

Afterlife

Breeder

The Children's Hour

Dark of the Eye

Goat Dance

The Halloween Man

The Hour Before Dark

Mr. Darkness

Naomi

Neverland

You Come When I Call You

NOVELLAS & SHORT NOVELS

The Attraction

The Dark Game (Two Novelettes)

Dinner with the Cannibal Sisters

Isis

The Necromancer

Purity

The Words

SERIES

THE HARROW SERIES

Nightmare House, Book 1

Mischief, Book 2

The Infinite, Book 3

The Abandoned, Book 4

The Necromancer

Isis

THE CRIMINALLY INSANE SERIES

Bad Karma, Book 1

Red Angel, Book 2

Night Cage, Book 3

THE VAMPYRICON TRILOGY

The Priest of Blood, Book 1

The Lady of Serpents, Book 2

The Queen of Wolves, Book 3

THE CHRONICLES OF MORDRED

Mordred, Bastard Son

COLLECTIONS

Lights Out: Collected Stories

Night Asylum

The Nightmare Chronicles

Wild Things

BOX SET BUNDLES

Bad Places (3 Novels)

Coming of Age (3 Dark Novellas)

Dark Rooms (3 Novels)

Criminally Insane: The Series (3 Novels)

Halloween Chillers

Harrow: Three Novels (Books 1-3)

Harrow: Four Novels (Books 1-4)

Haunts (8 Novel Box Set)

Lights Out (3 Collection Box Set)

Night Towns (3 Novels)

The Vampyricon Trilogy (3 Novels)

With more new novels, novellas and stories to come.

THE POISONER'S GARDEN & OTHERS

❦

For Raul
Who read them first
And lived a few.

❦

CONTENTS

Foreword   15

PART I
THORNY GRASP OF ROSES
1. The Poisoner's Garden   21
2. Why My Doll is Evil   27
3. The Salt of Undone Collars   31
4. Swimming in Underwear   33
5. Medea in Transit   49
6. My Younger Self   51
7. Toast to the Damned   53
8. Cenote of Dreams   55

PART II
HOURS AND DAYS
9. October Wind   59
10. On All Hallow's Eve   61
11. Song of Lupercalia   65
12. For St. Valentine's Day   69
13. On the Ides of March   71
14. Birthday   75
15. Winter Solstice   77
16. The Christmas Smite   79

PART III
STILL LIVES & ERRANT RHYMES
17. Elegy on a Frog Found Dead in   89
    Swimming Pool
18. At the Station in the Rain   91
19. Still Life   93
20. That Hardscrabble Life You're In   95

21. Assam Tea   97
22. The Crime   99

Afterword   101
About the Author   109

Foreword

Indulge me in this life of rhyme.

❦

Cenote, from the Mayan word, describes a natural limestone sinkhole or well, fed by subterranean rivers far below.

The first time I ever saw a photograph of a cenote was in *National Geographic* when I was a kid. About the same age, let's say ten or eleven, I read a book about Mexico that claimed the ancient Mayans tossed people as sacrifice into these holes during times of trouble

When I was eleven, I went with my family on a driving trip through Mexico and wound up visiting archeological sites all over the country.

I kept looking for those cenotes.

But would I leap?

❦

For those who missed all other warnings:

This volume in your hands is not a short fiction collection, except insofar as poetry can be fictitious.

❦

I write poetry when not digging into the shadow territories of fiction. I've always done this in one way or another, either composing them with music or just writing them without a tune in my head.

Many of these poems have at least a tinge of darkness to them and all of them have a story to tell. However, I weighted this book with the more serious poems upfront and the lighter or event-specific poems after.

❦

I divided them up into sections (*Thorny Grasp*

of Roses, Hours and Days, etc.) to prepare you for the mood or moments of where the individual poems best fit.

I hope you enjoy each one.

Douglas Clegg
    April 1, 2019

PART I
THORNY GRASP OF ROSES
From the Cenote of Dreams

The Poisoner's Garden

Among the thorny grasp of roses
Near aconite and pale foxglove
Far past the red anemone
'Neath fruiting manzanilla tree
At temple of Persephone,
Where lies my heart?
Where lies my love?

Below the ridge of mossy stone
My love met satyr in a mask
Who led him down a perfumed aisle
Among the lilies of the Nile
Off crooked path of chamomile,
While sipping ale from leaden cask.

As respite from a searing sun

To arbor, they, through colonnade,
On marble plinth the two entwine;
Wisteria snaking down the vine;
The shrouded faun
Failed to divine
One who spied from deepest shade.

I'd warned my love: Do not be fooled
By sweetened glance or siren's call,
Though honey drips below the hive
Its guardian stings
With poisoned knives
And stories of such ruined lives
Keep secrets at that garden wall.

I knew this satyr in disguise,
I'd heard such whispers in the town
Of lovers lost and rumored dead
At bleeding heart
And nightshade bed;
This creature steps upon the head
Of Venus, in her bath,
To drown.

But my innocent, my heart, my soul,
Sun-kissed eyes of bright larkspur
Returned at dusk from his meander
In burnished mood

With trifling candor
While in his hair, white oleander,
Betrayed a faithless saboteur.

Will you take me there, my love?
To yonder manzanilla tree
That weeps with sap of brutal venom
Among the sumac,
Mint, and lemon,
To ragged grove
That's meant to hem in
The temple of Persephone?

That marble dome to stolen bride,
Nearby a well of hemlock water,
On caryatids' shoulders press
A yoke imposed
By their mistress,
Whose shadow lets no light possess
The shrine of fair Demeter's daughter.

She, who strayed midsummer's noon
Unchaperoned at ancient well,
Torn from a pleasure garden's bloom,
Abducted by the ruthless groom,
Her deity: eternal gloom
Anointed at the throne of Hell.

This temple to the goddess dark
Who judges men, her winter chore,
As pomegranate trees surround,
Staining red
Her sacred mound.
She, wearing oleander crown,
Drapes her gown with hellebore.

So, there I drew him to that well
And tricked him to his crime confess
His gaze seemed not his own to me,
Eyes shaded with antimony,
I could not recognize who he
Became, after his sharp transgress.

We drank; I laughed; forgave him all,
Though he protested innocence.
We heard an owl in hunt disturbed
That ghostly, otherworldly bird,
With sound
That seemed a foreign word
Made chilling by its dissonance.

As violet light veiled poppy field
We lay beside that sacred well.
I roused him, yet no sound made he.
I kissed his eyes
That he would see

And offered him up humbly
At altar to the Queen of Hell.

Within deep thicket blossom's cup
Within each cup a drop of nectar,
Within each sip a poisoned sup,
As bees in swift vibration vector
Lured by hue with honeyed lies
Rush to sip this venom's nectar.
A serpent sting,
Its poison flies
And then my love,
My love he dies.

So him with his bright flowering smile
Lustrous gleam and glistened eyes
Inhales his last of chamomile
There, captured in the thorny pile
Along that verdant, fetid mile
Dies my love,
My love he dies.

A beauty grows from moldy earth,
Which empty flesh may fertilize,
To bloom beneath this mossy ridge
Where lies my love,
My love he lies.

Past prickly grip of hungry vine
Embraced in copperheaded nests
Of asphodel and baby's breath
Where every beauty tastes of death,
Where worm and beetle
Plumb the depth
Where beats my heart,
My heart here rests:

Among the thorny grasp of roses
Near aconite and pale foxglove
Far past the red anemone,
'Neath fruiting manzanilla tree
At temple of Persephone,
There lies my heart,
There lies my love.

Why My Doll is Evil

She came from Japan
In 1963;
My father, on business,
Saw her in a shop window.
With her fan and obi
And her curious smile,
She stood on a chest of drawers.

I could not sleep some nights
Looking at that placid face
So shiny and white
In the nightlight's halo.
She beckons and repels
With gently curved hand.
Her lips move at night
But she has no voice.

Things happen in houses
Where families live.

She watched,
And I watched her watch.
She smiled as it happened,
Held her fan close;
Her gaze told me nothing.
I watched her lips move
But she remained silent
While it happened.

Now in the attic
She rests,
Knowing more
Than she can say.

Her black hair is ragged,
Her obi, torn.
Her perfect feet
Tucked into wooden sandals,
Arthritic at her age.

Yet she smiles,
Holds her fan just so;
Without voice
Reminds me of

Things that happened
In families
While she stood
Watch.

The Salt of Undone Collars

There are points in time
When specific people come together
To vandalize chitinous shells
With ancient vulgar graffiti,
Forging pathways of deceit
Within that opaque well
Of shameful children
Whose bright futures
Clang loud and brassy
From an unseen depth
Where dissolved is
The salt of undone collars
Among the twisting hair
Of hyacinth root
Which smothers the sodden mattress
That once made your bed.

But long after,
With cupped hands,
From unimagined years
Of translucent want,
A sip.

Swimming in Underwear

When I turned nineteen I fell in bed
With a boy my age.
Should I call us young men?
Did not feel like it.
We were naive
And living underwater
Swimming in underwear
With the world above our heads;
Brilliant sunlight
Beyond our grasp.

We, in sepia pond,
Speaking
Through liquid
To those who peered down
From above

Wondering how we could live
Under the surface
And still manage to breathe.
But fish do it,
Turtles manage it for a time,
Eels, too.
Murky water-dwellers
Such as ourselves
Get by, below.

On a slender mattress
In narrow room
Wrapped around each other,
Drowsy pythons
Unwilling to unhinge jaws.
Talking in whispers,
Language couched in murmurs
With familiarity
And caution,
Breathy in undertow
So no one else might hear.
Others patrolled up and down
The hall outside
The narrow room.

I thought,
Is this what I think it is?
Is this even possible?

Why don't we talk about this?
Will my life be destroyed?
Whose fault is this?
Am I to blame?
He must be to blame.
I would never ordinarily do this.

Did I emit a signal?
The cosmic dog whistle
Of alien beings?
Did I seem too friendly,
Too ready,
Too willing?
Is it another reality?
Am I like those people,
The ones on late night talk shows,
The ones in parades,
The ones people make fun of?
The ones I feel bad for?
The ones in the papers
And in novels
Whose lives lead them
To tragedy
Or to Los Angeles
Or to opera?
Although all lives
It could be said
End in tragedy

But in the papers
And novels
Everyone else seems okay
Except men like this.
Can't be me.
Do I talk like them?
Is this what they do?

But no, thought I while wrapped
In unhindered warmth.
No, they're different.
Odder, stranger,
Another thing entirely.
We're simply possessed in some way
But it's a phase, a moment.
We can exorcise ourselves
Drive out the demons,
Reshape the clay of us
And be free.
And, anyway, every guy
Must have this going on,
This struggle.
They just don't mention it.

I wondered:
Am I his dirty secret?
Is he mine?
Do we live in two worlds or three?

Where we can exist, same as anyone
Yet different?
What would happen
If others found out?
Would they mock?
Want to beat us up?
Make jokes at our expense?
Rude hand gestures
To represent us?

Will we go insane from this?
Will life end?
Or worse,
Will we live in those ghettos
Of disco lights and glitter shoes?
And become lovesick waiters
Who are terribly witty
But a little sad;
Or think of poor old Oscar Wilde
In Reading Gaol
Doing hard labor
Of love
Despite all he gave to the world;
Or Truman Capote in fedora;
Or Gore Vidal and his glare;
Or the movie stars rumored;
Or the unknown legends
Of bathroom graffiti.

Or that guy a few blocks from home
In his early twenties
Who swims
In his underwear
Who glanced your way
Summer before
At the lake
Other side of the dock
Where cottonmouths
And eels
Hide beneath shadows of trees;
Or else you wished
He'd looked back as he swam.
Trapped by a rumor he was
Caught with some suburban father,
Or possibly breaking into a home,
Or something no one would mention,
Some vague, unspeakable
Act of depravity
That you could only
Long to imagine.
You want to end up like that?

Really the best option
Once one pulls oneself out
From the brackish pond
May be that lovesick waiter
Because he's at least off

In the city, in the ghetto,
In the places where those people go
To dance clubs
On the side of town
Where dangerous things happen
And no one's surprised by anything.
Is there nothing but doom ahead?
If anyone knew, could we survive?

When he abandoned me
To that bed, our little bed,
A bed made for spinal problems
With slender mattress
Holding up our six foot frames
Where he'd gently snore
Against my arm,
It felt deserved.

I slept in ice caves
Afterward.
Could not speak the language.
A wanderer in an unfamiliar world.
Others glanced at me as if
They thought they knew someone
That looked a bit like me
But could not possibly be
The same person.

My watery brethren called
From beneath pond scum:
Come on, come on,
You're missing out.
There's a secret hatch down here
And once you go through
You won't even care
About that world of sunlight
Where everyone else
Looks down at you.

I pretend not to hear them,
Those fractious sirens
From depth of cenote.
I know what they get up to.
It's all fun and games
Until you drown.

He, the first to leave our bed,
Figured out I'd been visiting
From another planet in disguise.
Not like him at all.
The bed had no meaning.
What a mistake that was.
A narrow escape
From a narrow bed,
He must have thought,
His unspoken words in my head

Loud and crashing,
Clear as water.

Perhaps I'd become invisible after all,
Way deep down below the surface.
Had I sunk
Among swaying grasses with eels
And dragonfly larvae?
I barely heard him
When he said:
You should never write about it.

About what?

What happened here.
You want to write
But promise me
You won't write about this,
The this that never was anything
Anyway.
And you're weird, he said.
He's weird, he told others.

And then, sometime later,
After a frozen year
In Washington,
Lost on rainy side streets
I chanced upon a smoker in tweed

Who offered me a cigarette
As we sheltered beneath an awning.

Gift accepted,
Though I didn't smoke;
Well, I only smoked
When others offered
The camouflage of tobacco.
Something about smoking
Still seemed cool;
Meant you were in on the joke;
More worldly than you looked
Even though I coughed
More than inhaled.

Was this nice stranger a professor?
Or just professed to it?
My father professor confessor,
Not old enough for that:
To me his age of nearly thirty
Seemed one broken hip away
From senescence.

He knew opera and drama;
Could quote Shakespeare;
Recite James Dickey;
In the next breath,
Eliot and Yeats.

He often sat
Opposite *Morning in the Tropics*
At the National Gallery
On wistful unhappy days.

He could yak about beauty and loss
And where you could get
The best Ethiopian food —
And with a British accent.
It was all I could do
To keep my shirt tucked in
And my button down
Buttoned up.

In the time it took to smoke
Two cigarettes
Beneath the awning
Out of the rain
On a dark end of Georgetown,
The downpour stopped.

We walked over a bridge.
I barely noticed the street.
His voice drew me in,
His glottals and iambs,
As he told me
How he broke the surface
And went places

Back and forth
Between worlds.

I wanted to inhale him
As he regaled me with
Histories of writers and actors
He'd known, and with bitter
But thrilling tone
Described their drab escapades.

None of them are what they seem.
But remarkable you, he told me,
You know what you want to be.
No one usually knows
Until they're much older.
Even then, they're not sure.
Someday you should write about this.

What 'this'?

All this, look around, me, you,
Cigarettes, Shakespeare, the rain,
It's poetry, each breath is poetry,
The way you smile is poetry, he said.

Like Shakespeare and Marlowe,
I said, imitating him,
And drab writers and actors

Who drearily debauch in daily
dalliances.

Let's go up, he laughed,
I have this book you might like.
You can borrow it.
I'm right over here
Across the street,
Used to be an embassy or something.
Don't be fooled by the regal facade
You American you,
Impressed by towers and moats
And dungeons.
It's all little rooms inside,
Though mine has a fireplace in it
So there's that
But not much else —
And my landlady's terrifying.

Will you look at that?
This world's going to Hell.
Will you just look at that guy?
Now that's just sad,
Show a little dignity.
He pointed at a mirror in the foyer
As he said this,
And that was when I knew
I would follow him

Up slippery marble steps.

I found myself once again
On a slice of bed
In a small room
Beyond which others patrolled halls.

One must be quiet
He warned
Hand over mouth if necessary.

Not that, I said,
Surely that's one step too far.
I glanced around his place
That could've been
A small office in an embassy,
Part of someone's mansion before that,
Now a boarding house
But with marble staircase
And tower rooms.

In the curious night
And blinding day
After,
When I let every wild thing
Inside me
Out
To dog paddle,

Australian crawl,
And nearly drown,
Despite anything between us
But the warmth,
I kept wondering about
Who this person was
Swimming in his underwear
Beneath whose skin
I existed.

By noon, I walked
Free of my demonic possession;
My prison;
Exorcised.
I side-stepped my way
Between worlds,
Jumping puddles and stones
Like some Devonian fish
Deciding forward or back,
Evolution or devolution,
Will you move into daylight?
Will you retreat
To the smothering mud?

Or like someone who
Lands on the moon
No longer sure
If Earth matters anymore

But continues, annoyingly,
To debate the question;
And if not yet entirely fluent
In the *lingua luna*
(A slow learner after all,
Though immersion
Might change that)
At least knowing your way
Around enough
To order coffee or beer
And get by.

Medea in Transit

Chopping arms
Legs
And their little heads
Tassels of hair flowing
Tunics torn
She sows the sea
With her brothers
And clings to one
Who will cut out her heart
All for a fleece
Of gold.

My Younger Self

❦

My younger self who is no more,
I hang his hat
Outside the door.
I throw his shoes into the bin
And warn him,
"Don't come back again."

No matter how I lock him out
He sneaks through cracks
Of timeless doubt
And tells old jokes at my expense,
Reminding me
Of accidents

And every time I played the dope
By clinging

To a hopeless hope,
Or turning left
When I should've right,
Or gambling hearts
All through the night.

Those golden hours so freely spent
(With little left to pay the rent.)
At these I laugh: The price of youth!
Then, he invokes
The most uncouth:

One hazy hour
When all seemed clear.
I knew the moment,
Recalled the year.
And there — a face —
From memories gray
When I did not say
What I longed to say.
I did not say
What I longed to say.
And now, is it any wonder I
Should wish
My younger self would die?

Toast to the Damned

I've damned myself to writing
And damned myself to play
I damn myself for sleeping in
When I might seize the day.

I've damned myself to middle age
From damned mishandled youth
And damn myself
With damning rhymes
In damned decrepitude.

Upon the damned shores of damn
We gather, we who chose our plan,
Ignoring those who better knew
The things
That they'd been told to do.

Let's raise a glass,
Who boldly squandered
And upon rocky cliffsides wandered
To choose the life of no esteem,
These arts
(Ungrateful, damned dream)
Or took the chance to be,
To be,
What others called frivolity.

But won't it be a little grand
To say:
We are,
We are the damned?

Cenote of Dreams

In Paris you made just one mistake
Which, when in London,
Failed to make.
Manhattan opened wide your eyes
While in L.A.,
You parted thighs.
In Washington, you found your way,
At suburb's slouch in disarray.

No matter where
You breathe or thrive
It's to that sinkhole
That you dive
Down deep
Deep down
Below the seams

Within the cenote of dreams.

Through limestone cave
Runs river dark
To endless sea of Kukulkan
From jaws to tail of serpent god
Across the lake of Acheron.

Returning to a well
Transcendent
You plunge head first,
A true descendant
From deep
Down deep
Through endless streams
Born from the cenote of dreams.

PART II
HOURS AND DAYS
Of Noted Occasion

October Wind

Winter, in the welcome guise
Of Summer's mask
And Autumn's cloak,
Shades sun against the clouded eyes,
Draws weary shoulders
Out their yoke.

She gilds each leaf,
Twists vine and bark,
Her gentle brush a death provoke,
Her lullaby a weeping lark —
Distraction from
The coming dark.

On All Hallow's Eve

In villages dark
When spies the night moon
On All Hallows' Eve
The witches festoon
Dim trees with bright lanterns
And with artful resolve
Beat drums to a mystery
No one can solve.

Riding moonlight and broomstick
(Cars, bikes – even more ways)
On All Hallows' Eve,
They abandon their doorways
And race to a meadow
At the deep forest clearing
Where their raucous wild music

Is just beyond hearing.

You may find yourself floating
Much to your surprise
On All Hallows' Eve
Out window, toward skies.

You set down in the midst
Of the witches bewitching
While they dance in a trance
Full of twisting and twitching.

"Here, drink golden mead,
And eat sweet cakes unfrosted."
On All Hallows' Eve
While your fears are accosted
But the faces, unmasked,
Are the ones from your childhood
As they spin in a circle
Amongst the thick wildwood.

As you drink and you sup
You may laugh with such violence
That you meet your true love
In a moment of silence;
Where the night seems a year,
While a year wanders aimless —
On All Hallows' Eve

Your behavior is shameless.

After sun breaches treetops
When night's all but dead
After All Hallows' Eve
You awake in your bed.
In the mirror's reflection
You find age in your glance,
No longer those bright eyes
From before the night's dance.

Wary neighbors will point
And warn young ones to heed,
"On All Hallows' Eve
You must not drink the mead,
Neither dance in the meadow
Nor love at such cost
Or you'll end up like this one,
All gray-haired and lost."

But ignore them and speak
Of those intrinsic riches
On All Hallows' Eve,
When you danced with the witches.

Song of Lupercalia

When cute little slogans
And heart shaped confections
No longer hold sway
Over lovers' affections;
When Valentine's Day, without fail,
Starts to fail ya,
Trade candy for nine-tails
And join Lupercalia.

Those cool ancient Romans
And the folks just before 'em,
Met in street, bar, and temple
To create quite a quorum
And they'd chase ya or otherwise
Try to assail ya

When they cracked their long whips
During fun Lupercalia.

So in mid-February
Don't whimper and moan
Because violets are blue
And you sit all alone;
Or you didn't get cards
Or your spouse is a bore,
Or no one remembered
To tell you "J'adore."
You could be lusting and laughing
While snapping your towel
Chasing nymph and wild satyr
Where ancient wolves howl.

Join Romulus and Remus
To carpe the diem
At the rip-roaring party
By the old Coliseum.

Just don't cry in your beer
Or regret in your tea,
You can join in the revels
At quarter to three.
When at last sets the sun
And the cops come to jail ya,
Tell 'em you got swept up in

Your first Lupercalia.

Yes, and when the moon rises
And your senses derail ya
Don't forget to get dressed
After wild Lupercalia.

For St. Valentine's Day

❧

For St. Valentine's Day
I rip out my heart
And beg young bully Eros
The use of a dart;

Please aim his damned arrow
At the casual lust
Of the one who once left me
Alone in the dust.

For St. Valentine's Day
I tear out my eyes
And — St. Lucy forgive me —
I offer this prize
To the one who avoided
My admiring gaze

In the long ago youth
Of my shallower days.

Let us drink to the saint
Who condemned us to this,
Feeling old at a bar
Sipping vodka and piss
Mingled with bitters
And blackberry brandy
While parades from the past
Open boxes of candy
With roses strewn in
Their ungrateful directions.
Oh, love, love, says I,
What a poisoned confection.

For St. Valentine's Day
I conjure the ghost
Of arm-entwined innocents
Warm-bedded as toast,
Hearts beating,
Eyes closing,
While dreaming of this:
The mirage of a life
In a lover's first kiss.

On the Ides of March

Recall the time when Julius Caesar
Heard prophecy
From some old geezer,
A sayer of sooth
With this strange teaser:
Beware the Ides of March.

On Senate floor, with Caesar seizing,
And Senators all 'round him,
Pleasing,
And Brutus – inside –
Burning, freezing,
The day: the Ides of March.

With drum beats, in their hearts,
Incessant,

Brutus and the others present
Played their parts,
Their play, unpleasant,
'Twas called "The Ides of March."

Then Caesar fell with swift unease,
Knives cutting
Through his symmetries
And meeting Death
Upon his knees
Sighed, "Ah! The Ides of March."

So question this,
If you would reason,
Why the god of war's wild season
In ancient Rome
Should cause such treason,
Accursed Ides of March?

Why the day known as the Ides?
Was it the moon
That drew the tides
Which forced these men
To take their sides
Upon that Ides of March?

Did Caesar hold the expectation
(Encouraged by the seer's narration)

His day had come,
The sweet cessation
Of breath, that Ides of March?

Or do such legends grow
From hindsight
To comfort us who hope to find light
While cowering
In humble blind-sight
Before our Ides of March?

Birthday

On this day one gets razzle-dazzled.
Wine may be drunk,
Nerves will grow frazzled.
Eschew the cake for macaroons,
Excuse yourself to watch cartoons
While people wander by and cheer:
Another year,
Another year,
And still, you're here.

Forget this moment of your borning
Rebirth another soft spring morning.
Remember eggs warm in the nest
Now on some diner's plate may rest
Or picture kisses borrowed, loaned,
The numbers that one never phoned,

Letters not responded to —
So much to do
The year's still new –
And yet, so few.

Recall instead the mother's joy
When first she held aloft her boy
That grew for months
In restless sleep
Sightless creature from the deep.

With labors meant for Hercules,
Her heart, when stopped,
Revived with ease.
She, Atlas, raising up the Earth:
Do not forget your hour of birth
Do not forget your hour of birth.

Winter Solstice

At dawn we shift the sand and mud
To find a passage haunted
By dark,
Beneath a granite sky
The eye remains undaunted.

Unfiltered memories sow discord.
Imagined voices rumors trade.
We dig up rock
And shift the sand
To make sense of this dark charade.

Conjure ghosts of brighter moments,
Summon shades from days of light
While hieroglyphs
Of turgid pomp

Guide us through this endless night.

When at last we strike a match
To view the resting place of days
No sarcophagus awaits us,
No mummy wrapped,
No bones to raise.

And yet despite this, here we are.
At dawn we hear the bleating cry:
The sun is dead,
The sun is dead,
And darkness owns the sky!

The Christmas Smite

When the wind howls like wolves
Leaping rooftop to shed
And the snow grows in silence
Like a whisper of dread,
Then rides that gnarly,
Disgruntled old troll
They call Christmas Smite—
And he hunts for your soul.

Yes, he carries a sack
Just for stealing your spirit,
The fire inside you —
He can smell when he's near it.
He drives a wild team
On his shadowy way
With six feral cats

All pulling his sleigh.
(And none of them like him,
These cats in their nooses,
But they must do his bidding
For magic he uses;
And if even one feline
Smite's temper arouses,
He will transform them all
Into little gray mouses.)

Now Smite is not handsome
Nor is his face placid;
His eyes are like pennies
Left too long in acid.
His chin, rough and rotted,
His nose like a dart,
His whiskers all prickly —
And so is his heart.
But back to his face,
It seems so incomplete
And his breath can kill spiders
At twenty-one feet!
His two-pointed hat,
All crushed, slouches low
And it jingles
With little round bells he loves so —
The effect of it all,
From his bow to his beam,

Is of an evil court jester
Whose jokes make you scream.

He rides the wild night
With his yowling swift crew
Till he comes to the window
Of someone – like you.
Then he climbs up the wood
Or shingle or brick
Up the side of your house
Like a self-loathing tick.
He can make himself tiny
Or huge if he chooses
And he'll wait to break in
When you're deep in your snoozes.
Then inside he slips,
With the stealth of a slug
Leaving a trail of slime on your rug.

As a troll, he's a climber
For he usually dwells
In cavernous chasms
Down deep in dark wells
Which he crawls up each year
For his winter's bonanza
Whether Solstice or Hanukkah,
Christmas or Kwanzaa.
No matter to him whether girl,

Woman, man, boy —
He comes to steal souls
Of those who've lost joy.

To climb up your bed sheets
And shimmy the post
Is nothing to him,
This Smite who would boast
"I could climb highest towers,
I could swim deepest seas!"
So he leaps to your toes
And then hops to your knees.
While you're lost in your snoring
And dreaming and rambles,
Up to your face
This little troll scrambles.
He stands on your earlobe
Leaning in very bold
And whispers the dangerous magic
Of old.

Then a whimpering sound
Escapes from your lips.
You might feel a trembling
Right down to your hips.
In your dreams you might fall
From a mountain in Spain
Or find yourself drowning

Within Lake Champlain,
Or even, perhaps, you've been
Thrown from a mare —
But it's all just a dream,
Still you're not quite aware
That the old Christmas Smite,
Your soul he now purges —
His sack at the ready
For when it emerges.

Now, some say
The soul looks like nothing at all
And other say "light,"
Still others "a ball,"
But I've heard from someone
Who woke to the Smite
That the soul looks like mist
From the river of night.

Still, no one alive
Remembers quite how
The soul leaves the body,
But I'll tell you right now:
All the Smite's victims
Wake up the next morn
And they've lost every memory
Of where they were born.

Sure, they go to their schools
Or their jobs, as they're able,
But when you are sitting
With them at the table
You'll notice that
Something seems blank
In their eyes,
They don't laugh at jokes,
And they never seem wise,
And they refuse to like ice cream,
Or puppies, or kites.
In fact, some of them even
Resemble these Smites.

So if you would avoid
A villainous Smite
Then hang onto your joy,
Your sense of delight
No matter how mournful
Life may become,
No matter your task,
No matter how glum.
When you're hit with bad news,
Don't just fall apart —
On the coldest of days,
Keep a fire in your heart.
That odd Christmas Smite
Can do nothing to those

Whose joy is alive
Clear down to their toes.

But if you allow
Your joy to die out
If bad days destroy you
Or fill you with doubt,
And any stubbed toe
Or hangnail brings fury,
Or a boss or a teacher
Or a kid or a jury
Makes you feel small
Or tries to annoy --
Even so, *let no one steal your joy.*

For joy itself lightens the dark
When your heart's at its lowest,
You fire up that spark.
If you allow it to die —
And not just in this stanza —
But on evenings like Christmas
Or Solstice or Kwanzaa
Or Hanukkah, too,
Well, you get the gist,
That old bitter troll
Will put you on his list.

When the wind howls like wolves

Leaping rooftop to shed
And the snow grows in silence
Like a whisper of dread,
Then rides that gnarly,
Disgruntled old troll
They call Christmas Smite —
And he hunts for your soul.

PART III

STILL LIVES &
ERRANT RHYMES

A Miscellany

Elegy on a Frog Found Dead in
Swimming Pool

Oh frog, warrior among the lilies:
In powerful rains you lost your way.
Crystal waters endless
Called you from your murky lair.

How it must have seemed the sea
Beyond Elysium,
Infinite and shining.
Halfway across you swam
And there, I netted you.

Your funeral rites were brief.
You rest now in the gully
Watched over by a rabbit of bronze
Alongside tall grasses,
Beneath gray stones.

May you swim among
The hyacinth of paradise.

At the Station in the Rain

Nearby a tall man stains his shirt,
A woman may have torn her skirt,
A poet sits with soul inert
And scribbles lines of trains and dirt.

Not one of these would ever hurt
With answer so unjust and curt
Putting me on high alert
That you are not
Who once you were't.

But am I still
The one who said
Better bad
Than good and dead?
When one day found

I'd lost the thread
And you with smile
But not a shred
Of kindness
Nodded your fine head
And gave sly glance (for once)
Instead
Of saying what you felt,
Abed.

Now, no men mind a shirt with stain
No skirt-torn ladies e'er complain,
Yet poets pen their worst quatrains
Invoking dirt and tracks — and rain.

While on a bench of wooden pain
I wait for an approaching train
That brings its metal death-refrain:
The rhythmic pressure of your name.
Your name, your name, your name.

Still Life

Lemons captured in a bowl.
Painted plates upon the pine.
A water hyacinth left whole.
Carafes for breathing out the wine.
Percussive locusts in the trees.
Friends gather, first course,
Salads served
While crickets play their symphonies
And I sit by, somewhat unnerved.
Napkin stained by drops of wine,
In lantern light
Glance friend to friend
Who suffer under blade and tine —
One table, summer without end.

That Hardscrabble Life
You're In

You may choose the life of whimsy
Or pick to win, to win,
Each dawn you face
The soundtrack of
That hardscrabble life you're in.

Dog-eat-dog sing we, the miners
Scraping knife and teeth and coin,
Digging deep in earth
For reasons
To festoon the active groin.

No one engraved your obligation,
Nobody strapped you to the hour
Yet since crib you cry for playthings
From that spacious,

Specious bower.

And your cry brings tin-pan music
As you wildly dance and spin
"Put your little foot,
Put your little foot"
To that hardscrabble life you're in.

But if you choose the life of whimsy
If you face it with a grin
Then the needle lifts
And hovers over
That hardscrabble life you're in —

And you laugh within that silence
Far beyond the grinding din
From rusty old machinery of
That hardscrabble life you're in.

Assam Tea

You can keep your opium,
Your crack cocaine and e,
There's no addiction finer than
A cup of Assam tea.

Even giant old Goliath,
Though no body left had he,
One thing that Philistine desireth:
A cup of Assam tea.

While Cleopatra sorely tested,
In bed her Antony,
A single tribute was requested:
A cup of Assam tea.

Those flags that Alexander furled

Before age thirty-three?
Would he have conquered
Half the world
Without his Assam tea?

And so I raise a cup at ease
For those who follow me.
You want to write
Bright rhymes like these?
Drink your Assam tea.

The Crime

In the wake of a terrible rhyme
Flows a heinous,
Unconscionable crime;
Murdered conventions
Of linguistic pretensions
With peculiar inventions
To squeeze more declensions
From line, to line, to line,
To line, to line,
To line.

Afterword

I should state upfront:

I never poisoned anyone in a garden by a temple of Persephone. Of course, that doesn't make it untrue down deep in the cenote of dreams.

Some of these poems are drawn up from my own memory.

But with a limestone cavernous twist.

☙❦☙

I believe in poetry — with or without rhyme.

I've written it since childhood and there has not been a stage in my life where I stopped even for a short time. It's always been a private thing for me although I've put a few poems online over the years and included a couple in story collections.

These various poems, rhymes and lines came into being over a range of several years. Most were drawn from specific incidents and direct observation — except for a few, including the poem whose title christens this collection.

❧

"The Poisoner's Garden" felt more like a conjuration than writing. I conceived a story and thought it would be prose, so I began writing but the words kept moving into a specific rhythm that moved me to speak them aloud as I wrote each one.

Rather than overcomplicate a simple tale of murder, love, mythology, and botany, it went to rhyme.

I realized the rhythms suggested a classical bent. Given my love for Persephone, whose bust guards an edge of our garden at home, well, there we are.

Speaking of that garden, one thing I've learned over the past half-dozen years of overseeing unruly tangles of botanical difficulty is that nearly everything beautiful that grows in the dirt is poisonous in some aspect. So the backyard itself inspired this poem as did my love for myth and classical poetry.

We grew some beautiful foxglove at some point but I kept worrying that neighbors' pets might find the blossoms dropped on the ground and decide to ingest them. Never happened, but it was on my mind.

As if with telepathy and an unwillingness to stay where not wanted, the foxglove decided not to appear ever again.

"The Poisoner's Garden" is a tale about a man speaking directly of his sense of betrayal, passion — and murderous jealousy — for his lover, also a man.

But it's about something else, too, having to do with beauty, love, possession, nature, power, sex, and the dark beneath the daylight.

A subterranean sea, if you will.

※

It's this great dark underground sea within which treasures of shipwrecks may be found and from which sea monsters arise.

As I've grown older, it's that deep sea that calls me most and which I resist at times.

A handful of these poems come directly from those expeditions.

❧

The direct first person narrators here are rarely me, but there are exceptions.

"Why My Doll is Evil," has a basis in fact in terms of a doll that my father bought in Japan for my older sister sometime between 1958 and 1962 or thereabouts.

I found that doll creepy but she was also beautiful and mysterious. She stood there on my sister's dresser that faced the open door to her room. If I had to walk by on the way to my parents' room or browse the hallway book case I might briefly glance through the doorway.

There she stood, holding her fan.

I've always found dolls unnerving at best.

That doll is a relic sunk to the sea floor. In recalling it, another story suggested itself.

"The Salt of Undone Collars" might seem enigmatic but it's as much about layers of self including the "opaque well" of memory versus the clarity longed for by the one remembering the promises, crashes, and coded realities of childhood versus the first awakening moments in adulthood (and sometimes, with some of us, the second awakening moments); where everything gets thrown together into the depth until you plunge down to the one moment, a brief flash of minute or hour, that you wish to isolate and — for a second or two — revive and draw up from the confusion.

Plus, water hyacinth — which does a remarkable job of cleaning pond water of impurities so you can see all the way down through the depths. We have a fish pond and those beautiful weedy purple flowers with Rapunzel roots do a great filtering job even while they crowd out other plants.

"Swimming in Underwear" may be the most directly autobiographical poem in this collection, although time, people, and place were changed because, well, one does that to protect the innocent...and we all were innocent and guilty in this.

If you're reading this and you think you might have been a player in the drama of this poem, it's not you.

It never was you.

The poem speaks for itself but I feel it represents the moment when a person makes a major leap into life based on what's known from the inside-out despite every unfounded fear and opposing viewpoint foisted from the outside-in.

With "Birthday," my mother's heart stopped during my birth and she *was* revived with ease, or more specifically with a needle.

My mother also dreamed while giving birth that I would go in the ocean someday and be killed by a shark.

There's that deep sea again.

Her dream, told to me many years later, made sense of why she seemed overly worried when she watched me play in the surf as a child.

Years later, a friend told me that it wasn't something to be afraid about because likely that dream meant the shark was my guide and not my destroyer.

I still haven't written a poem about this, but I might.

I continue to be cautious around oceans and hope my guides aren't hunting me when I venture out.

The depths are dark and vast, after all.

And yet, one leaps.

Some poems come from the surface with a

slight dip below, but without any deep sea diving.

A handful are drawn from mild daily musing ("Assam Tea," "Still Life,") and observation ("At the Station in the Rain.")

"The Christmas Smite" arrived because I believe that you can lose everything in life but once you lose your sense of joy, you've lost all. Additionally, I wanted to write about a creepy little nasty troll who may have escaped Santa's mad elf asylum.

The final poem, "The Crime," is simply laughing at myself for my unfettered love of poems that rhyme.

And that's as much as I'll say here regarding these poems.

I'm off to go for a dive in the ol' cenote.

Douglas Clegg
April 10, 2019

About the Author

Douglas Clegg is the *New York Times* bestselling and award-winning author of *Neverland, The Priest of Blood, Afterlife,* and *The Hour Before Dark,* among many other novels, novellas and stories. His first collection, *The Nightmare Chronicles,* won both the Bram Stoker Award and the International Horror Guild Award. His work has been published by Simon & Schuster, Penguin/Berkley, Signet, Dorchester, Bantam Dell Doubleday, Cemetery Dance Publications, Subterranean Press, Alkemara Press and others.

A pioneer in the ebook world, his novel *Naomi* made international news when it was launched as the world's first ebook serial in early 1999 and was called "the first major work of fiction to originate in cyberspace" by *Publisher's Weekly,* covered in *Time* magazine, *Business Week, Business 2.0, BBC Radio, NPR, USA Today* and more. His book *Purity* was the first to be published via mobile phone in the U.S. in early 2001.

He is married, and lives and writes along the coast of New England.

Find the Author Online:
www.DouglasClegg.com

facebook.com/DouglasClegg

twitter.com/DouglasClegg

bookbub.com/authors/douglas-clegg